Flight or Fright?

by Janine Scott

illustrated by Olivier Daumas

OXFORD
UNIVERSITY PRESS
AUSTRALIA & NEW ZEALAND

OXFORD
UNIVERSITY PRESS

Oxford University Press is a department of the University of Oxford.
It furthers the University's objective of excellence in research,
scholarship, and education by publishing worldwide. Oxford is a registered
trademark of Oxford University Press in the UK and in certain other countries.

Published in Australia by
Oxford University Press
Level 8, 737 Bourke Street, Docklands, Victoria 3008, Australia

First published 2014
This edition 2019

ISBN 9780190317959

Series Editor: Nikki Gamble
Designed by Oxford University Press in collaboration with Fiona Lee, Pounce Creative
Illustrated by Olivier Daumas
Printed in China by Leo Paper Products Ltd
Links to third party websites are provided by Oxford in good faith and for information only.
Oxford disclaims any responsibility for the materials contained in any third party website referenced in this work.

Acknowledgements

The publishers would like to thank the following for the permission to reproduce photographs:

p4–5: Bettmann/Corbis; **p9b**: DIZ Muenchen GmbH, Sueddeutsche Zeitung Photo/Alamy; **p8–9**: Bettmann/Corbis;
p10–11: Corbis; **p11b**: Bettmann/Corbis; **p13**: RGB Ventures LLC dba SuperStock/Alamy; **p14–15**: Popperfoto/Getty Images;
p16–17: Time & Life Pictures/Getty Images; **p18–19**: Popperfoto/Getty Images; **p19b**: PF-(sdasm1)/Alamy; **p20–21**: CNP/
Sygma/Corbis; **p22–23**: REX

We have made every effort to trace and contact all copyright holders before publication. If notified, the publisher will
rectify any errors or omissions at the earliest opportunity.

Contents

Fly Like Birds

Long ago, people wanted to fly. They climbed up high, put on wings and flapped – and then they jumped! They usually landed in a heap.

Since then, people have made many different flying machines. It took lots of **trial and error** before humans built a machine that could fly.

Testing the machines was often **trial** *and* TERROR!

The birdman flying machine was one
of the earliest flying machines.

Fear in the Air

In 1783, French brothers Joseph and Jacques Montgolfier designed a large hot-air balloon. They built a fire on the ground and held the opening of the balloon over the fire.

The balloon went up, but the smell was terrible – they had put old shoes and rotten meat on the fire!

Trial and error

The Montgolfier brothers got their balloon idea when they saw paper scraps floating near a fire. To test their idea, they filled paper bags with smoke.

Trial and TERROR!

The brothers were afraid to test the balloon themselves, so they sent a sheep, duck and rooster up instead! Luckily, the animals landed safely.

Glider Rider

A glider is a flying machine that has no engine. Its specially shaped wings help it glide through the air.

Otto Lilienthal was a German glider inventor known as the "Glider King". In 1894, Otto built a big hill, which he used to **launch** his gliders.

Otto Lilienthal flew his first glider in 1891.

Trial and error

Otto made at least nine different gliders. Over five years, he went for more than 2000 glider flights.

Trial and TERROR!

On 9th August 1896, Otto crashed his glider. Sadly, he died from his injuries the next day.

Otto Lilienthal

9

Fiery Flight

Airships are big balloons with bags of gas inside them. This gas is lighter than air, so it helps the airship rise. The first airships were filled with **flammable** gas.

Trial and error

In early airships, the bags that held the gas were made from cows' **intestines**. The intestines of 250 000 cows were needed for one airship!

The *Hindenburg* was a huge airship. It had a dining room and a lounge.

The *Hindenburg's* first flight was in 1936.

Trial and TERROR!

The *Hindenburg* exploded in 1937. Sadly, many people onboard died.

Sky Flyer

On 14th December 1903, the first **powered** aeroplane took flight – and then crashed! The *Flyer*, which was built by the Wright brothers, flew for just 3.5 seconds.

Three days later, the *Flyer* flew again – this time for 12 seconds, at Kitty Hawk in the United States of America (USA). Kitty Hawk was a good place for flying. It had strong winds, which helped the *Flyer* take off, and soft sand for crash landings!

Trial and error

The Wright brothers built a **wind tunnel**. They used it to test about 200 different wing shapes.

The *Flyer* took its first proper flight on 17th December 1903.

Trial and TERROR!

The Wright brothers flew the *Flyer* three more times after the first flight. After its fourth flight, a big wind flipped the *Flyer*, damaging it. It never flew again.

Wooden Wonder

Most aeroplanes today are made of metal. However, the *Mosquito* was made of wood. It was designed in England and flown during World War II. It was one of the fastest aeroplanes flown in the war.

The plane was held together with screws and glue. When the *Mosquito* flew in hot places, the glue sometimes came unstuck!

Trial and error

In England during World War II, furniture makers and piano makers helped make the planes!

The *Mosquito* was first flown in 1940.

Trial and TERROR!

One of the *Mosquito*'s nicknames was the "**Timber** Terror".

Floating Flyer

A flying boat is a plane that can land on water. The biggest flying boat ever built was the *Spruce Goose*. It was made out of wood. Most people thought it was too big to fly.

The *Spruce Goose* took its first and only flight on 2nd November 1947.

The *Spruce Goose* was designed to carry 750 soldiers during World War II. Unfortunately, it wasn't ready in time!

Trial and error

The *Spruce Goose* flew only once, for less than one minute! It was never used again.

17

In a Spin

Helicopters fly up, down, backwards, forwards and sideways. They can even hover in one place.

Helicopters have two **rotors** that spin around – a main rotor and a tail rotor. Without a tail rotor, a helicopter would turn in circles!

Igor Sikorsky made the first successful American helicopter in 1939.

tail rotor

Trial and TERROR!

Igor's first helicopter went backwards and sideways. However, it had trouble going forwards!

Trial and error

Igor made so many changes to his helicopter design, it was nicknamed "Igor's Nightmare"!

main rotor

Igor Sikorsky first flew his helicopter
on 14th September 1939.

Invisible!

The B-2 stealth bomber is a warplane. It was designed in secret and first flew in 1989. It has a smooth shape and special paint that make it almost impossible for **radars** to find.

Trial and error

Sometimes B-2s drop dummy bombs. These look like bombs, but they do not explode. They are used during training exercises.

The B-2 stealth bomber is painted grey, which makes it hard to see in the sky.

Trial and TERROR!

Some B-2 flights are 40 hours long. There is a toilet in the plane, but there are no walls around it!

Space Plane

SpaceShipTwo is a plane designed to take tourists into space. It went on its first powered test flight in April 2013.

A plane called *WhiteKnightTwo* carries *SpaceShipTwo* into the sky and lets it go in mid-air. *SpaceShipTwo* then flies into space.

A flight will last about 2.5 hours, but the tourists will be in space for only a few minutes. In space, there is no gravity to pull things towards the ground. So the people can float around inside the plane!

Trial and error

SpaceShipTwo's first test flight was not in space. It was over a desert.

SpaceShipTwo

WhiteKnightTwo

Trial and TERROR!

SpaceShipTwo can re-enter Earth's **atmosphere** at any angle – even upside down!

Glossary

atmosphere: the layer of gas and cloud around Earth

flammable: likely to catch fire easily and burn quickly

intestines: long tubes under the stomach which help to move food through the body

launch: to start something moving

powered: moves with the help of an engine

radars: machines that use radio waves to find objects

rotors: the spinning parts of a helicopter; the main rotor helps the helicopter to lift off the ground

timber: wood

trial and error: to keep trying, and learning from your mistakes, until you are successful

wind tunnel: a huge tube with air moving inside it

Index